Meander into the Curious World of
TURTLES

Published by Wildlife Education, Ltd.
12233 Thatcher Court, Poway, California 92064
contact us at: **1-800-477-5034**
e-mail us at: **animals@zoobooks.com**
visit us at: **www.zoobooks.com**

ISBN 1-888153-99-7

Turtles

Series Created by
John Bonnett Wexo

Written by
Timothy Levi Biel

Editorial Consultant
John Bonnett Wexo

Scientific Consultants
Dr. Peter C.H. Pritchard, Ph.D.
Florida Audubon Society

Dr. Jeanne Mortimer, Ph.D.
Zoological Department
University of Florida

Contents

*T*urtles are strange-looking creatures. The shells on their backs are like roofs that they carry with them wherever they go. No other animals in the world have shells quite like these. The shell has been the secret of the turtle's success for millions of years.

Like dinosaurs, turtles are primitive reptiles that first appeared on earth about 200 million years ago. These early turtles had smaller shells than most modern turtles. The small shells left the turtles' heads exposed. As dangerous predators began to appear, many turtles gradually developed larger shells that allowed their heads to fit inside.

Today, dinosaurs no longer roam the earth. But turtles keep plodding along, mostly unchanged over the years. Their shells give them excellent protection, and this has helped them adapt to all but the coldest parts of the world. They live in jungles, mountains, rivers, deserts, and in the sea.

There are more than 200 different species of turtles in the world. They range in size from tiny speckled tortoises, which weigh less than one-half pound, to monstrous leatherback turtles, which can weigh 1,500 pounds! Most of these species fit into one of three main groups—freshwater turtles, sea turtles, or tortoises.

Freshwater turtles live in rivers or ponds. They have webbed feet and flat shells. Sea turtles live in the sea and have powerful flippers for swimming long distances. Tortoises are a special group of turtles that live on dry land. Most of them have shells that are dome shaped. They have thick, heavy legs for walking.

A few turtles do not fit any of these groups. They swim like freshwater turtles, but they spend a lot of time on land, like tortoises. Scientists call these turtles *semi-terrestrial*, which means, "partly land dwelling." They are also known as *terrapins*.

Some species of turtles probably live near you. You can find them living in a local pond or in some nearby woods. If people don't disturb them, they can live there for a long time. Some turtles live to be 100 years old.

A **turtle's shell** is part of its skeleton. It cannot be removed from the turtle's body any easier than you could remove *your* skeleton from *your* body. What makes the turtle's skeleton so different is that its ribs and backbone are attached to flat, bony plates.

These plates form a wonderful shelter that surrounds the turtle's body and keeps it safe from predators.

Of course, this skeleton also shapes the rest of the turtle's body. For example, its legs must stick out sideways in order to fit beneath the shell. With its bowed legs and bulky shell, the turtle is very slow and awkward, at least on land.

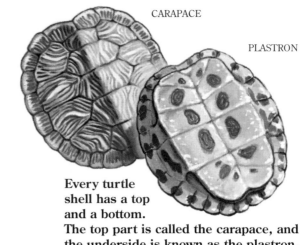

CARAPACE

PLASTRON

Every turtle shell has a top and a bottom. The top part is called the carapace, and the underside is known as the plastron.

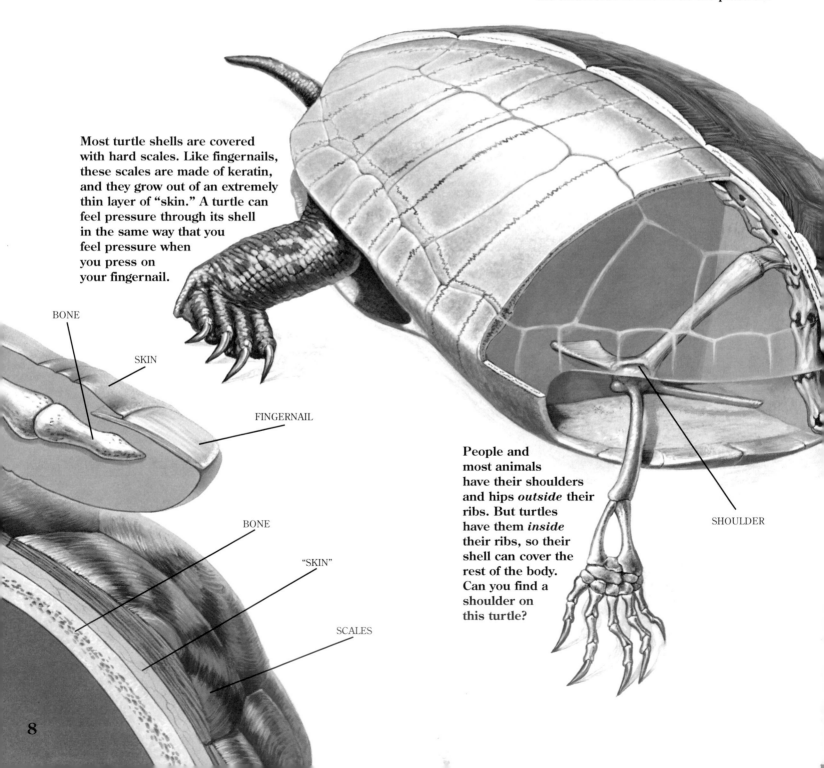

Most turtle shells are covered with hard scales. Like fingernails, these scales are made of keratin, and they grow out of an extremely thin layer of "skin." A turtle can feel pressure through its shell in the same way that you feel pressure when you press on your fingernail.

BONE

SKIN

FINGERNAIL

BONE

"SKIN"

SCALES

People and most animals have their shoulders and hips *outside* their ribs. But turtles have them *inside* their ribs, so their shell can cover the rest of the body. Can you find a shoulder on this turtle?

SHOULDER

Turtle shells are not all alike. Some can close completely around the head and body, while others can't. A tortoise's shell, for example, barely fits over its head, so its face is not protected.

DESERT TORTOISE

A turtle's legs may move slowly, but its neck can move with lightning speed. The neck muscles are extremely flexible, and the skin is very loose. This allows the turtle to pull its whole neck inside the shell in case of danger.

To pull their heads under their shells, most turtles fold their necks in an "S" shape, as shown at right.

For its size, the sea turtle has a very small shell. It barely covers the turtle's back and provides no protection to the head or legs.

HAWKSBILL TURTLE

Turtles have no teeth. But their jaws have a hard covering, just like a bird's beak. The edges of these jaws are very sharp, so that turtles can eat many different kinds of food. The painted turtle, at left, is using its jaws to chop leaves.

The jaws of every turtle look different. Some have sharp points that are used like teeth for grabbing prey. Mexican mud turtles may use these points to grab frogs.

9

Soft-shelled turtles, like this pig-nosed variety,
have flat, round shells covered with leathery
skin instead of horny plates. They have tube-
shaped noses that they use like snorkels in
rivers of North America, Africa, and Asia.
Soft-shells are fierce-natured and fast. They
are meat-eaters that live mostly on fish.

Fresh water is the place where most turtles live. There are many different kinds of freshwater turtles in the world. Some of them are tiny, like the little spotted turtles that are often sold in pet shops. Others can get quite large, like the snapping turtles shown here.

These turtles find most of their food in the water. Many of them eat fish and other animals, which they catch in a number of different ways. Big snapping turtles, like the one at right, sometimes even try to sneak up on ducks.

Freshwater turtles can be found in warm tropical streams as well as in northern ponds that may freeze in the winter. This is remarkable because turtles—like all reptiles— are *cold-blooded*. In other words, their body temperatures rise and fall with the temperature of their surroundings. So freshwater turtles must use their surroundings in many ways to keep from getting too hot or too cold.

TERRAPIN

Like you, turtles have to breathe air. But they don't need nearly as much oxygen as you do. In fact, a turtle can stay underwater for hours without breathing!

On sunny days, turtles climb out of the water to warm up on rocks or logs. When they get too warm, they dive back into the water.

On cold days, the water may be warmer than the land, so the turtles stay in the water. If the water itself gets too cold, they dig burrows in the mud. Inside their burrows, turtles may go into a deep sleep that lasts for months.

The carapace of a matamata turtle may reach 18 inches. The turtle's triangular head and neck extend well beyond its shell. This strange-looking turtle from South America hides in murky water, where its reddish color and its unusual shape blend into the surroundings. When unsuspecting fish swim by, the matamata sucks them in like a vacuum cleaner. It stretches its long neck and opens its huge mouth. Water and fish are pulled in, and the water is expelled. The matamata's long nose lets it breathe above water while its body stays submerged.

The common snapping turtle is only about half as large as its cousin, the alligator snapping turtle, but it is a more aggressive hunter. It has extremely powerful jaws, and once they close around an animal, there is no escape. This allows the snapping turtle to capture large fish—and even ducks, occasionally.

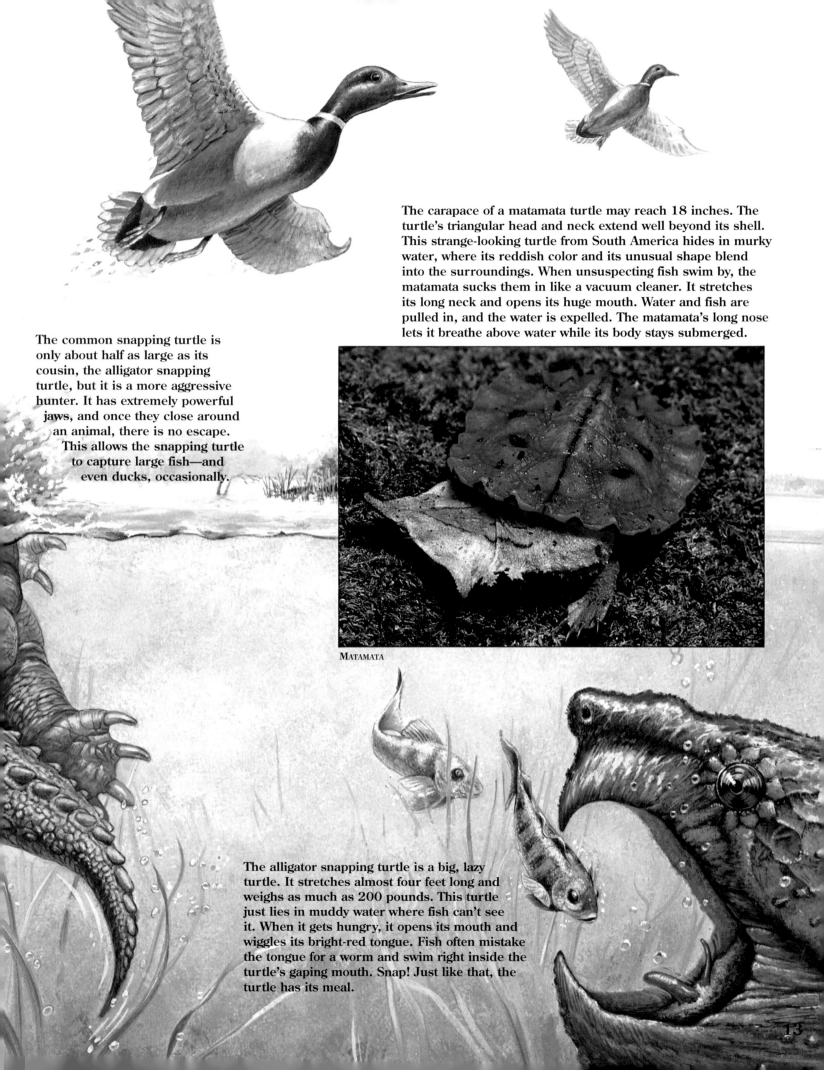

MATAMATA

The alligator snapping turtle is a big, lazy turtle. It stretches almost four feet long and weighs as much as 200 pounds. This turtle just lies in muddy water where fish can't see it. When it gets hungry, it opens its mouth and wiggles its bright-red tongue. Fish often mistake the tongue for a worm and swim right inside the turtle's gaping mouth. Snap! Just like that, the turtle has its meal.

Desert tortoises enjoy the desert flowers that bloom in the spring as much as people do. While people are happy to see the colorful cactus flowers, the turtles are glad to *eat* them!

Tortoises are even slower than most other turtles. It takes a tortoise five hours just to walk one mile! But it doesn't need to move any faster.

It doesn't have to run fast to find food, because it eats plants. With its shell to protect it, it has no fear of predators. Most tortoises live in dry places where it helps to move slowly. If they tried to carry their heavy shells any faster, tortoises would just get hot, tired, and thirsty.

Tortoises usually lead slow, quiet, and peaceful lives. There is very little that frightens or excites them. Occasionally, however, male tortoises get excited enough to fight over a female, as the two desert tortoises are doing below.

GIANT LAND TORTOISE

Most tortoises weigh less than 10 pounds. But a giant land tortoise may weigh *600 pounds*! That's about as heavy as three large men.

Watching two male tortoises fight is like watching a movie in slow motion. The tortoises push each other with their shells until one of them gets tipped on its back. A fight like this may last for hours.

16

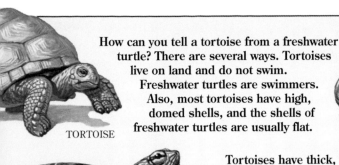

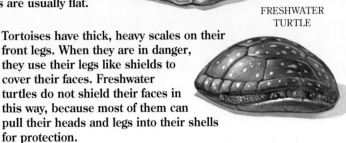

How can you tell a tortoise from a freshwater turtle? There are several ways. Tortoises live on land and do not swim. Freshwater turtles are swimmers. Also, most tortoises have high, domed shells, and the shells of freshwater turtles are usually flat.

TORTOISE

TORTOISE

FRESHWATER TURTLE

Tortoises have thick, heavy scales on their front legs. When they are in danger, they use their legs like shields to cover their faces. Freshwater turtles do not shield their faces in this way, because most of them can pull their heads and legs into their shells for protection.

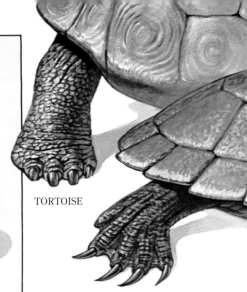

TORTOISE

FRESHWATER TURTLE

Freshwater turtles have thin, flat legs that are built for swimming. Tortoises have round, sturdy legs for walking on land. Because they live on land, tortoises do not have webbing between their toes like freshwater turtles do. Finally, a tortoise's back foot has only four toes, while a freshwater turtle's has five.

LEOPARD TORTOISE

Many animals cannot survive in dry places because they can't find enough water. But tortoises get all the water they need by eating cactus and other plants that store moisture.

DESERT TORTOISES

In a fight, the tortoise that gets tipped over loses. If it can't get back on its feet, it could lose its life! Left out in the hot sun, a tortoise will quickly get too hot and die.

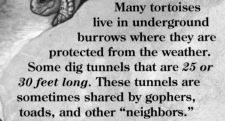

Many tortoises live in underground burrows where they are protected from the weather. Some dig tunnels that are *25 or 30 feet long.* These tunnels are sometimes shared by gophers, toads, and other "neighbors."

Mysterious sea turtles have been roaming the world's oceans for millions of years. They were there at the time of the dinosaurs, and they are still there today. Yet until recently, scientists knew very little about them. They were rarely seen except when they came to shore to mate and lay their eggs. Then they disappeared again into the sea.

However, with the aid of modern radio and satellite equipment, scientists are beginning to solve some of the mysteries of the sea turtle. They now know that these turtles travel in regular migration routes, some of them for thousands of miles. Every two or three years, they return to the same beaches where they hatched as babies. There are still sea turtle mysteries to be solved. No one knows how these turtles can make such long voyages and still find their way back to the same beaches time after time.

Millions of years ago, the ancestors of sea turtles lived on land. Today, sea turtles are completely adapted to life at sea. For example, the bones that once formed the turtle's toes have become extremely long. Instead of forming separate toes, they work together to form a big flipper.

PACIFIC RIDLEY TURTLES

Near a beach in Costa Rica, thousands of Pacific ridley turtles arrive at about the same time every year to mate. When all the females haul themselves onto shore to lay their eggs, they practically cover the whole beach! They may even do this in the daytime, although like most sea turtles, they usually lay their eggs at night.

Many turtle shells have beautifully colored scales. But none are as thick and durable as the hawksbill turtle's (above). For this reason, people use its scales to make tortoiseshell combs and jewelry. Unfortunately, for hundreds of years there were no limits on hunting these beautiful sea turtles. Today, they are seriously endangered.

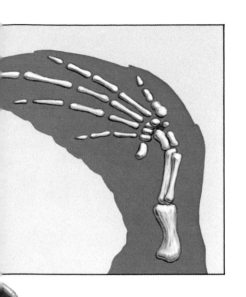

Sea turtles
have changed very little
since the days when dinosaurs roamed the earth.
The leatherback turtle (above) looks a lot like its
ancestors (shown below).

ARCHELON

As far as we know, the largest sea turtle that ever lived was *Archelon*. Scientists have found skeletons of this giant sea turtle that have carapaces about 12 feet long. It is estimated that this prehistoric sea turtle from North America weighed about 4,000 pounds. *Archelon* was about the size of a small car!

Sea turtles can "fly" through the water. They are such powerful swimmers that some can reach speeds up to 20 miles per hour. That's about 100 times faster than a tortoise can walk!

Sea turtles get a lot of salt from the ocean water they drink.

GREEN TURTLE

If they take in too much salt, they might die. To get rid of the extra salt, sea turtles shed big, salty tears.

A sea turtle's shell does not cover its head and legs. This makes it easier for the sea turtle to swim, but takes away some of its protective "armor." Instead of a larger shell, the sea turtle has thick, scaly skin on its head and legs. This skin protects it like a leather coat and hood.

19

A **young turtle's life** is full of danger. Like most reptiles, it gets no protection from its mother. In fact, it never sees her. The mother turtle buries her eggs in the ground and leaves them to hatch by themselves. Many of the eggs will not hatch, however, because animals and people find the eggs and eat them.

The baby turtles that do hatch are called *hatchlings*, and they face even more problems. On these pages, you will see how baby sea turtles hatch and the dangers that await them. The first thing the hatchlings must do is dig their way out of an underground nest. This may take a few days, or even *a few weeks*! Then they must find their way to the sea. Before the hatchlings reach the sea, hungry predators catch many of them. Even when they reach the sea, they are not safe from ocean predators.

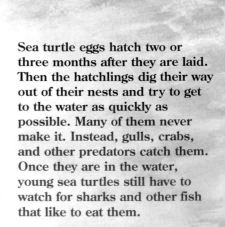

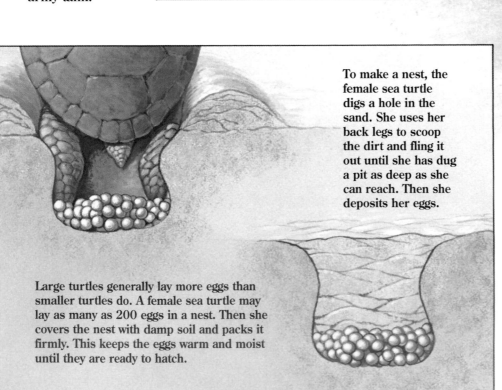

A mother sea turtle comes ashore long enough to lay her eggs and cover them up. Then she returns to the sea. Sea turtles are very awkward on land. They can only move by dragging their heavy bodies over the sand, leaving a trail that looks like it was made by an army tank!

To make a nest, the female sea turtle digs a hole in the sand. She uses her back legs to scoop the dirt and fling it out until she has dug a pit as deep as she can reach. Then she deposits her eggs.

Large turtles generally lay more eggs than smaller turtles do. A female sea turtle may lay as many as 200 eggs in a nest. Then she covers the nest with damp soil and packs it firmly. This keeps the eggs warm and moist until they are ready to hatch.

Sea turtle eggs hatch two or three months after they are laid. Then the hatchlings dig their way out of their nests and try to get to the water as quickly as possible. Many of them never make it. Instead, gulls, crabs, and other predators catch them. Once they are in the water, young sea turtles still have to watch for sharks and other fish that like to eat them.

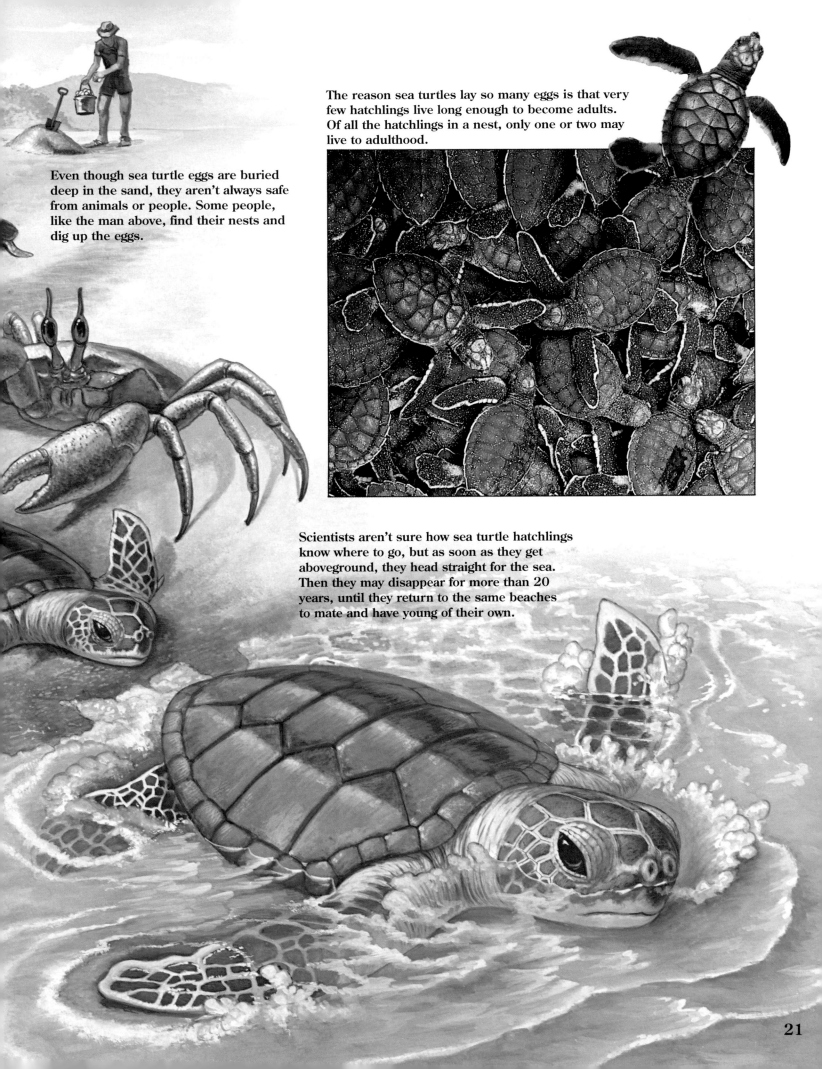

Even though sea turtle eggs are buried deep in the sand, they aren't always safe from animals or people. Some people, like the man above, find their nests and dig up the eggs.

The reason sea turtles lay so many eggs is that very few hatchlings live long enough to become adults. Of all the hatchlings in a nest, only one or two may live to adulthood.

Scientists aren't sure how sea turtle hatchlings know where to go, but as soon as they get aboveground, they head straight for the sea. Then they may disappear for more than 20 years, until they return to the same beaches to mate and have young of their own.

21

The future of turtles once seemed secure. For millions of years, their shells were the only protection they needed. Today, they also need the protection of people. Turtles face many of the same problems that other wild animals face. Some have been overhunted, while others are threatened by pollution, habitat destruction, and the loss of important food sources.

Giant tortoises were numerous in the Galapagos Islands and the Seychelle Islands 200 years ago. Sailing ships made regular stops in the Galapagos, where their holds were loaded with tortoises to supply food for the ships' crews. This exploitation and the eventual introduction of feral animals to the islands resulted in a great loss of tortoises. Goats scour the islands to eat the food that the tortoises eat, while rats and pigs feast on the tortoises' eggs and young. The giant tortoise from Aldabra Island is the only giant tortoise that remains in the Seychelles.

All giant tortoises are considered to be threatened species. In fact, 96 species of turtles, tortoises, and terrapins are threatened. Some are vulnerable, some are endangered, and some are critically endangered.

Sea turtles are sought for their meat, eggs, shell, and oil. Whether accidental or intentional, thousands upon thousands of sea turtles are caught by longline fishermen every year. Many other thousands are caught in drift nets. Ocean pollution and oil spills also take their toll. Development of nesting beaches for human use can destroy habitat and drive turtles away from their historic nesting places. All species of sea turtles are endangered, two of them critically so.

People can make a difference in the lives of wild animals—for good or for bad. Thousands of people work in conservation programs as professionals or volunteers in order to save sea turtles. Much of the work takes place on the nesting beaches, where turtles are monitored, measured, and tagged. There are others who help hatchling sea turtles find their way to the sea. Hatchlings headed for the sea can be confused by the bright lights of a beachfront hotel. When this happens, the hatchlings often head in the wrong direction.

Tourists vacationing on some of the tropical islands that attract turtles have been known to flock to the beach to turn wayward turtles in the right direction. Without the help of many individuals and organizations, sea turtles may be destined for extinction.

Loggerhead turtle

23

Index